FABULOUS DESSERTS

MAINLY MICROWAVE

OTHER NO NONSENSE COOKING GUIDES

OTHER NO NONSENSE GUIDES

NO NONSENSE COOKING GUIDE

FABULOUS DESSERTS

MAINLY MICROWAVE

IRENA CHALMERS

LONGMEADOW PRESS

FABULOUS DESSERTS: MAINLY MICROWAVE

Copyright © 1987 by Irena Chalmers

Published by Longmeadow Press, 201 High Ridge Road, Stamford, Con-
necticut 06904. No part of this book may be reproduced or used in any
form or by any means, electronic or mechanical, including photocopying,
recording, or by an information storage and retrieval system, without
permission in writing from the publisher.

ISBN 0-681-40270-9

Printed in the United States of America

0 9 8 7 6 5 4 3 2

STAFF FOR NO NONSENSE COOKING GUIDES

EDITORIAL DIRECTION: **Jean Atcheson**

MANAGING EDITOR: **Mary Goodbody**

COVER DESIGN: **Karen Skelton**

ART DIRECTION & DESIGN: **Helene Berinsky**

RECIPE DEVELOPMENT: **Marilyn Schanze, Cynthia Salvino**
AMERICAN COOKING INSTITUTE, ST. JOSEPH, MICHIGAN

ASSISTANT EDITORS: **Mary Dauman, Dorothy Atcheson**

PROJECT MANAGER: **Nancy Kipper**

COVER PHOTOGRAPH: **Gerald Zanetti**

TYPESETTING: **ComCom, Allentown, Pennsylvania**

PRODUCTION SERVICES: **William S. Konecky Associates, New York**

CONTENTS

ACKNOWLEDGMENTS

Grateful acknowledgment is made to the following for permission to reproduce or adapt original recipes:

The Almond Board; California Tree Fruit Agreement; California Raisin Advisory Board; California Strawberry Advisory Board; Castle and Cooke Foods (Dole); Chambord Liqueur; Corning Glass Works; Dixie Crystals; Foreign Vintages, Inc. (Amaretto de Saronno); The Golden Delicious Apple Growers of Washington; Hershey Foods Corporation; National Peach Council; The Peanut Advisory Board; Ms. Jane Stacey; Virginia State Apple Commission; Washington Apple Commission

FABULOUS DESSERTS: MAINLY MICROWAVE

How many times have you scanned the dessert section of a menu first? Or planned a dinner party around a magnificent dessert? Or stopped for a second look at a magazine with a glorious cake on the cover? Desserts are glamorous, exciting, indulgent and ever-so-slightly wicked. Which is why almost everyone loves them.

Desserts come in every sort of shape and form—cookies, cakes, pies, candies, puddings and so on—but they all share one feature: sweetness. Not all desserts are *super* sweet, of course. A bowl of June's best strawberries, embellished with nothing more than the afternoon sunshine, is a sublime dessert. Equally sublime is a dish of homemade ice cream topped with creamy hot fudge sauce and sweetened whipped cream, or a slice of chocolate swirl cake, or a generous wedge of lemon meringue pie, or several peanut butter cookies.

We find ourselves thinking of desserts and sweets when we plan holiday celebrations and birthdays. We also think of them when we put together an ordinary weekday supper or pack a lunchbox. A little something sweet after any meal sits well with the palate as well as the soul.

Perhaps the simplest desserts are cookies, bars and brownies. These morsel-sized confections are easy to mix and bake and can be stored in a tin for instant satisfaction—with a cup of coffee after supper or as an afternoon pick-me-up.

Pies and cakes are all-American favorites that remind us of the rich variety of our ethnic roots. We make pies from seasonal fruits and berries, relishing the arrival in the stores of peaches, plums, nectarines, cherries, strawberries and apples. We also make them from sweet creams and custards, nuts and chocolate and ice cream. Our favorite pies are nestled in flaky crusts and topped with sweet crumb toppings or clouds of meringue.

Our favorite cakes are usually frosted with generous swirls of buttercream, confectioners' sugar icings or flavored whipped cream. Plain pound cakes and spicy fruit and nut cakes are equally loved, and often need no frosting. A dusting of confectioners' sugar, a liqueur-spiked raspberry syrup or a spoonful of hard sauce does very well, instead.

Beyond cookies, pies and cakes are puddings, custards, mousses and all manner of fruit-based desserts. Smooth, satisfying and often intensely flavored, puddings, custards and mousses appeal at the same time to our memories of childhood and our adult tastes. Fruit desserts give us room to indulge our penchant for baking and cooking with seasonal fruits and berries.

Many of these recipes are designed for the microwave, but not all. Sprinkled throughout every chapter is a generous handful of desserts that are more successfully made by conventional cooking methods. The microwave is outstanding when it comes to making puddings and custards, sauces and toppings. Many cakes and cookies do better in a slower oven where they can brown. When you are preparing these recipes or some of your old favorites, think of the microwave when you are called on to melt chocolate and butter, or heat sauces and glazes.

Whether you choose to make a dessert in the microwave or not, treat yourself to sweets. Many desserts are elaborate creations that require an afternoon's work; just as many are simple and quick. All are among life's pleasures.

USING YOUR MICROWAVE

MICROWAVE POWER AND TIMING

Most microwaves run on 600 to 700 watts, although some of the smaller models are less powerful. The recipes in this book have been developed for microwaves within this range but if yours is less than 600 watts, you will need to extend slightly the cooking times given in recipes.

Microwave cooking is not an exact science, so you cannot depend on time alone to determine when the food is cooked. Open the oven door during cooking to check the food for doneness and adjust times and power settings accordingly, just as you would in a conventional oven.

Remember: The amount of power can also be affected by various factors, such as use of other electrical equipment on the same circuit or even utility company procedures.

The temperature, size and shape of the food will affect the timing, too. Food at room temperature cooks more quickly than food just taken from the refrigerator.

POWER SETTINGS

Most of today's microwave ovens offer variable power settings ranging from High (100 percent power) to Low (10 percent). The higher settings are most often used for cooking or reheating, while the low settings are designed for simmering, defrosting or keeping food warm. Throughout this book, we have indicated the power percentage necessary for every recipe.

EQUIPMENT

You do not need any special utensils for basic microwave cooking, although as you become more adventurous you may want to invest in some of the equipment specially designed for the microwave, such as browning dishes or racks.

You cannot use metal containers, most aluminum foil, or even plates with a metallic trim because microwaves cannot pass through metal. If you put metal in the microwave, the waves will bounce off the metal and "arc," which means they will spark and sizzle. In some modern ovens, however, lightweight aluminum foil may be used for shielding parts of the food that might otherwise overcook.

Heatproof glass plates and dishes are ideal, as are most ceramics, porcelain or pottery. Test any utensil you are unsure about before using it in the microwave.

TESTING FOR "MICROWAVABILITY"

Put the utensil in the oven along with a 1-cup glass measure filled with tap water. Microwave on High (100 percent power) for 1 minute. If the dish remains cool while the water in the measure becomes hot, the utensil is safe to use, or "microwavable." If the dish becomes hot, it is absorbing microwave energy and should not be used. (During cooking, the transfer of heat from food *can* make microwavable dishes hot, so be sure to have potholders handy.)

MICROWAVE COOKING TECHNIQUES

Small, uniformly shaped pieces or amounts of food will cook more quickly than large. Shield the thinner parts of unevenly shaped foods to prevent overcooking.

Stir or rearrange food once or twice during the cooking process to help it cook more evenly. Rotating foods in the oven will achieve the same result.

Remember: Standing time is often part of cooking. Some foods will not seem completely cooked when removed from the microwave but the standing time will complete the process.

Use paper towels and plates, transparent wrap and wax paper in the microwave according to the recipe instructions. Dry plain white paper towels prevent spattering and absorb moisture. Wax paper makes a loose cover to hold in heat.

When a tight cover is needed to hold in steam and tenderize and cook food more evenly, use a casserole lid or transparent wrap rolled back slightly at one edge to allow for venting. Be careful of escaping steam as you remove a cover.

CHAPTER 1

COOKIES, BARS AND BROWNIES

Nearly everyone likes to bake cookies, bars and brownies. And certainly everyone likes to eat them fresh from the oven. Recipes specially developed for the microwave are so simple and quick that you can have warm and fragrant goodies in a matter of minutes. How better to please unexpected company or a hungry Little League team?

Bake only as many cookies as you need and save the rest of the dough in the refrigerator. No special baking equipment is required. Just use heatproof, microwavable glass dishes for the bars, and microwavable plates or wax paper for the cookies. It couldn't be easier.

REMEMBER!

Baked goods cooked in the microwave will have as good texture and flavor as those baked in conventional ovens, but they will not be brown and crisp.

This is most noticeable with light-colored cookies and cakes, so you may want to frost them or dust them with a sprinkling of confectioners' sugar or chocolate curls.

Lemon Squares

Makes 1½ dozen

Lemon bars are always popular and these, made in the microwave in a matter of minutes, are especially flavorful and chewy.

6 tablespoons (3 ounces) butter, softened
¼ cup packed brown sugar
⅛ teaspoon salt
¼ cup quick-cooking rolled oats
1 cup plus 3 tablespoons all-purpose flour
2 large eggs
¾ cup sugar
1 tablespoon grated lemon rind
1 tablespoon lemon juice
¼ teaspoon baking powder
Confectioners' sugar

Warm a lemon by microwaving on High (100 percent) for 25 to 40 seconds. You will find it yields more juice.

Beat the butter with the brown sugar and the salt until the mixture is fluffy. Stir in the oats and 1 cup of flour.

Pat the dough onto the bottom of an 8-inch square microwavable baking dish and set it on an inverted dish. Microwave on Medium (50 percent) for 4 to 6 minutes, rotating the dish a quarter turn every 2 minutes until set.

Beat the eggs with the sugar, the remaining 3 tablespoons flour, lemon rind, lemon juice and baking powder until the ingredients are thoroughly combined. Pour the mixture over the baked dough. Microwave on High (100 percent) for 3 to 4 minutes, rotating the dish a quarter turn every minute until the topping is set. Allow to cool completely.

Sift the confectioners' sugar over the top. Cut into 1-by-2-inch bars.

Chocolate-Frosted Cereal Squares

Makes about 6 dozen

Crunchy and sweet, these squares will find favor with children, whether they make them themselves or discover a couple tucked into the lunchbox.

For more chocolate flavor, try baking with chocolate chunks instead of chips. Chop your favorite semisweet chocolate bar into pieces and add these when the recipe instructs you to add the chips.

4 tablespoons (2 ounces) butter
4 cups miniature marshmallows
¾ cup creamy peanut butter
5 cups puffed rice cereal
½ cup peanut butter chips
½ cup semisweet chocolate chips
½ cup chopped unsalted peanuts

Put the butter in a 2-quart glass measure. Microwave on High (100 percent) for 45 seconds. Add the marshmallows and stir until they are coated with butter. Microwave on High (100 percent) for 2 minutes, stirring after 1 minute.

Add ¼ cup of the peanut butter and stir to blend. Add the cereal and stir until it is coated. Pour the mixture into a buttered 9-inch square microwavable pan.

Put the peanut butter chips, chocolate chips and ½ cup peanut butter in a 1-quart glass measure. Microwave on High (100 percent) for 1 minute and stir until smooth. Drizzle half of the chocolate mixture over the cereal and sprinkle with the peanuts. Drizzle the remaining chocolate mixture over the peanuts.

Cool until the chocolate is firm, then cut into 1-inch squares.

Ginger Cookies

Makes 3 dozen

Making these spicy ginger cookies is a snap in the microwave. They are baked a few at a time, arranged in a circle to promote more even cooking.

> 2½ cups all-purpose flour
> 2 teaspoons baking soda
> 1½ teaspoons cinnamon
> 1 teaspoon powdered ginger
> ½ teaspoon ground cloves
> 1 cup packed brown sugar
> ¾ cup vegetable shortening
> ¼ cup molasses
> 1 large egg
> ½ cup granulated sugar

Stir together the flour, baking soda, cinnamon, ginger and cloves.

Put the brown sugar, shortening, molasses and egg in a large bowl and beat until well combined. Stir in the dry ingredients and mix thoroughly. Form the dough into 1-inch balls and roll them in the granulated sugar.

Line a paper plate, baking rack or glass plate with wax paper. Arrange 5 balls of dough in a circle, spaced 2 inches apart and put 1 ball in the center.

Microwave on Medium (50 percent) for 1½ to 1¾ minutes, rotating the plate a half turn after 1 minute, until the surface of the cookies is no longer glossy. Remove the cookies and wax paper from the plate and set them aside to cool. Microwave the remaining cookies in the same way.

Chocolaty Chocolate Chip Bars

Makes 16

These bars pack a double whammy: chocolate chips are baked into the batter *and* melted on top as frosting.

> 8 tablespoons (4 ounces) butter, softened
> ¾ cup packed brown sugar
> 1 teaspoon vanilla extract
> 1 large egg
> 1¼ cups all-purpose flour
> 1 teaspoon baking soda
> ½ teaspoon salt
> 1¼ cups semisweet chocolate chips

Beat the butter with the sugar and vanilla until the mixture is fluffy. Add the egg and beat well.

Stir together the flour, baking soda and salt. Blend them thoroughly into the butter mixture. Stir in ¾ cup of the chocolate chips.

Spread the mixture evenly in an 8-by-8-inch glass baking dish. Protect the corners from overbaking by arranging 4 small squares of lightweight aluminum foil diagonally in each corner. Set the baking dish on an inverted plate.

Microwave on High (100 percent) for 1½ minutes, rotating the pan a quarter turn after 45 seconds. Remove the foil squares. Microwave on High (100 percent) for 1½ to 2½ minutes, rotating the dish every 45 seconds. The bars are done when the center springs back when lightly touched. (The moisture on the surface will dry during standing time.)

Sprinkle the remaining chocolate chips over the hot bars. Let stand for 10 minutes, then spread the melted chips evenly to frost. Cool and cut into bars.

Fudgy Brownies

Makes 16

These brownies are even more chocolaty if frosted with the Chocolate Frosting on page 43. But no one will blame you if you eat them almost as soon as you take them from the oven—they are so good you may not want to bother about the frosting!

> 2 ounces unsweetened chocolate
> 8 tablespoons (4 ounces) butter, cut into pieces
> 1 cup packed brown sugar
> ¾ cup all-purpose flour
> 2 large eggs
> ½ teaspoon baking powder
> ½ teaspoon vanilla extract
> ¼ teaspoon salt
> ½ cup finely chopped nuts (optional)

Combine the chocolate with the butter in a microwavable bowl. Microwave on Medium (50 percent) for 2 to 2½ minutes, until melted. Add the sugar and stir until well blended. Let the mixture cool slightly.

Add the remaining ingredients to the chocolate mixture and beat until well blended.

Lightly butter an 8-inch-square microwavable glass baking dish. Spread the mixture in the dish and microwave on High for 5 to 8 minutes until a toothpick inserted near the center comes out clean. Rotate the dish a quarter turn after 2, 4 and 5 minutes.

Cool the brownies in the dish and then cut them into 2-inch squares.

Always let bars and brownies sit for a few minutes before cutting them into squares.

Cocoa Brownies

Makes 14 to 16

These are ideal for unexpected guests. Cocoa powder is a staple in most kitchens and you will probably have all the other ingredients on hand, too.

Baked-in-the-round Cocoa Brownies have a less fudgy, more cakelike texture than the Fudgy Brownies. They are especially good served topped with ice cream and chocolate sauce.

4 tablespoons (2 ounces) butter
2 tablespoons vegetable shortening
6 tablespoons unsweetened cocoa powder
1 cup sugar
2 large eggs
½ teaspoon vanilla extract
1 cup all-purpose flour
¼ teaspoon baking powder
¼ teaspoon salt
½ cup chopped nuts

Combine the butter and the shortening in a glass mixing bowl and microwave on High (100 percent) for 1 minute, until melted.

Add the cocoa and stir until smooth. Stir in the sugar. Add the eggs and the vanilla and beat well. Stir in the flour, baking powder, salt and nuts.

Spread the batter in a lightly buttered 8-inch round glass baking dish, or pie plate. Microwave on Medium (50 percent) for 5 minutes, rotating the dish a quarter turn halfway through baking. Microwave on High (100 percent) for 2 to 3 minutes, until the brownies are puffed and dry on top. Cool until set and then cut into wedges.

Blonde Brownies

Makes 16

Just what they say they are, with a butterscotch flavor. Some people call them Blondies.

> 8 tablespoons (4 ounces) butter, cut into pieces
> ¾ cup packed brown sugar
> 2 large eggs
> ¾ cup all-purpose flour
> ½ teaspoon baking powder
> ½ teaspoon vanilla extract
> ¼ teaspoon salt
> ¼ cup chopped nuts
> ½ cup semisweet chocolate chips
> Confectioners' sugar

Place the butter in a microwavable mixing bowl and microwave on High (100 percent) for 45 to 60 seconds, until melted. Stir in the remaining ingredients, except the chocolate chips.

Lightly butter an 8-inch-square microwavable glass baking dish. Spread the mixture into the dish and sprinkle with half the chocolate chips. Shield the corners of the dish with squares of lightweight aluminum foil.

Microwave on High (100 percent) for 4 minutes, turning after 2 minutes. Remove the foil shields and sprinkle with the remaining chocolate chips.

Replace the foil and microwave on High (100 percent) for 1 to 3 minutes, rotating the dish a quarter turn every minute. Remove from the oven and discard the foil.

If you like, you can gently spread the melted chips over the brownies to make a thin glaze. When they are cool, sprinkle them with confectioners' sugar and cut into 2-inch squares.

Peanut Butter Chip Chocolate Cookies

Makes 2½ dozen

Peanut butter and chocolate are timeless favorites, and in combination they taste even better than apart.

8 tablespoons (4 ounces) butter, softened
¾ cup sugar
1 large egg
1 teaspoon vanilla extract
1 cup all-purpose flour
⅓ cup unsweetened cocoa powder
½ teaspoon baking soda
¼ teaspoon salt
6 ounces peanut butter chips

Combine the butter, sugar, egg and vanilla in a bowl and beat until the mixture is light and fluffy.

Combine the flour, cocoa, baking soda and salt. Stir them into the butter mixture. Stir in the peanut butter chips. Chill the dough for 30 minutes, until it is firm enough to handle.

Break off small pieces of the dough and shape them into 1-inch balls. Place 10 dough balls in a circle around the edge of a microwavable plate covered with wax paper. Flatten them slightly with the back of a fork. Microwave on Medium (50 percent) for 3½ to 4½ minutes, rotating the plate a quarter turn every minute. Cool the cookies for 5 minutes before removing from the plate.

Microwave the remaining cookies in the same way.

CHAPTER 2

PIES

S et a freshly baked pie on the table, and chances are there will be no leftovers. Pies seem to be as popular when listed on the menus of the most expensive restaurants as they are when waiting, in generous wedges, under glass domes in coffee shops and diners across the land. A piece of pie has an appeal that never fails.

Out of necessity, ingenuity and the desire for something sweet, Americans have long been concocting pies. Some are made from locally grown fruit and vegetables, others are filled with custard or meringue, and more modern formulas include ice cream. Some have top crusts as well as bottom crusts and some have sweetened crumbs sprinkled over them instead of a crust.

Whatever the crust and filling, pies are as welcome with a mid-morning cup of coffee as after a full-course dinner. And if there *are* any leftovers, a wedge of pie makes a terrific midnight snack.

21

Lemon Meringue Pie

Serves 6 to 8

It takes such a short time to put together the filling for this light, tasty version of the classic American pie, you will want to make it over and over again.

Buying some already-made frozen pie shells is a good time saver. Stock up so that you can put together a pie at a moment's notice.

1¾ cups sugar
⅓ cup cornstarch
⅛ teaspoon salt
1½ cups boiling water
3 large eggs, separated
1 tablespoon butter
½ cup lemon juice
2 tablespoons grated lemon rind
9½-inch baked pie shell, cooled
¼ teaspoon cream of tartar

DECORATION:
Grated lemon rind
Twisted lemon slices

Combine 1½ cups of the sugar with the cornstarch and salt in a 1-quart glass measure. Add the boiling water, whisking constantly until the mixture is smooth. Microwave on High (100 percent) for 2½ minutes or until thickened.

Lightly beat the egg yolks and add some of the hot mixture to them, stirring constantly. Stir the warmed egg yolks back into the rest of the hot mixture. Stir in the butter.

Microwave on High (100 percent) for 2 minutes, stirring after 1½ minutes. Stir in the lemon juice and the rind. Cool the mixture to room temperature and then pour it into the baked pie shell.

Using an electric mixer, beat the egg whites with the cream of tartar until foamy. Gradually add the remaining sugar, beating until the whites are stiff but not dry.

Spread the meringue over the lemon filling in the pie shell, covering the edges. Decorate with grated lemon rind and twists of lemon.

Crumb-Topped Apple Pie

Serves 6 to 8

Always a favorite, this pie can be whipped up in a few minutes. The sweet crumbly topping is made with oats, nuts and whole wheat flour.

6 cups peeled, sliced apples
1 tablespoon lemon juice
¾ cup packed brown sugar
2 tablespoons all-purpose flour
1½ teaspoons cinnamon
⅛ teaspoon mace
9½-inch pie shell, baked and cooled
¼ cup quick-cooking rolled oats
¼ cup whole wheat flour
¼ cup chopped walnuts or pecans
4 tablespoons (2 ounces) butter

Put the apple slices in a large bowl and toss with the lemon juice. Add ½ cup brown sugar, the flour, ¾ teaspoon of the cinnamon and the mace, and mix well.

Spoon the apple mixture into the pie shell.

Combine the oats with the whole wheat flour, nuts, the remaining ¼ cup brown sugar and ¾ teaspoon cinnamon. Add the butter and work it into the mixture with your fingertips until the mixture is crumbly. Sprinkle the crumbs over the apples.

Microwave on High (100 percent) for 8 to 10 minutes, just until the sugar and butter begin to melt.

Chocolate Cookie Crust

Makes 2 9-inch pie crusts

This crunchy pie crust can be the base for any number of different-flavored fillings, as well as the Chocolate Bar Pie.

> *8 tablespoons (4 ounces) butter*
> *1 cup sugar*
> *1 large egg*
> *1 teaspoon vanilla extract*
> *1¼ cups all-purpose flour*
> *½ cup unsweetened cocoa powder*
> *¾ teaspoon baking soda*
> *¼ teaspoon salt*

Beat the butter with the sugar until the mixture is light and fluffy. Add the egg and the vanilla and beat well.

Combine the flour, cocoa, baking soda and salt and stir them into the butter mixture.

Shape the dough into 2½-inch-thick rolls. Wrap them in wax paper and then in transparent wrap. Chill for several hours or overnight.

Cut one roll into ⅛-inch slices. Arrange them with the edges barely touching on the bottom and sides of a buttered 9-inch glass pie plate. Microwave on Medium (50 percent) for 5 to 6 minutes, rotating the plate a quarter turn every 2 minutes, until set. Cool completely before filling.

Repeat with the other roll, or freeze it to bake at another time. Or slice it, and make cookies.

CHOCOLATE COOKIES

Cut the roll of dough into ¼-inch slices. Arrange 10 slices in a circle on a sheet of wax paper and microwave on Medium (50 percent) for 4 to 5 minutes until just set, rotating a quarter turn every 2 minutes. Cool slightly, and sprinkle with sifted confectioners' sugar.

Chocolate Bar Pie

Serves 6 to 8

Chocolate lovers will fall for this rich, creamy and *very* chocolaty concoction.

> *8-ounce milk chocolate bar, broken into pieces*
> *⅓ cup milk*
> *1½ cups miniature marshmallows*
> *1 cup heavy cream*
> *9-inch Chocolate Cookie Crust, cooled*

Put the chocolate pieces in a glass mixing bowl. Add the milk and the marshmallows. Microwave on High (100 percent) for 3 to 4 minutes, stirring after 2 minutes, until the mixture is thick and smooth. Let it cool completely.

Beat the cream until it is stiff. Fold it into the chocolate mixture. Spoon the filling into the crust, cover with transparent wrap and chill thoroughly before serving.

Ice Cream Pie

Serves 8

Top-grade French
vanilla ice cream
is available
commercially—
just be sure the
ingredients list on
the package
includes fresh
cream, eggs and
vanilla.

A stunning combination of rich ice cream and rum-soaked glacéed fruits, heaped into a pie shell and topped with whipped cream—mmmmm! For a really special occasion, make the ice cream yourself.

> ½ cup mixed glacéed fruits, such as cherries,
>   pineapple, orange and lemon peels
> ⅓ cup rum or brandy
> 1½ quarts French vanilla ice cream
> 9-inch pastry shell, baked

> DECORATION:
> 1 cup heavy cream
> 2 tablespoons sugar
> 1 teaspoon vanilla extract

Chop the glacéed fruits and put them in a bowl. Add the rum or brandy and soak for 20 minutes.

Remove the ice cream from the freezer and let it sit at room temperature until it is the consistency of whipped cream. Fold the glacéed fruits and rum into the softened ice cream.

Transfer the ice cream mixture to a deep 8-inch pie plate. Cover and freeze until firm. Run a warm knife around the ice cream, invert a flat plate over the top and unmold it. Lay the ice cream in the 9-inch pie shell. (You may have to use two spatulas to lift it in.)

Pour the heavy cream into a chilled bowl and beat until slightly thickened. Add the sugar and continue beating until thick. Beat in the vanilla extract.

Fit a pastry bag with a star tip, half fill it with the cream and pipe rosettes around the ice cream pie. Or, if you prefer, use 2 spoons to decorate the top of the pie with whipped cream.

Applesauce Meringue Pie

Serves 8

> 2 large eggs, separated
> 4 cups applesauce
> ½ cup packed brown sugar
> 1 tablespoon grated lemon rind
> ⅛ teaspoon salt
> 9-inch deep-dish pastry shell, baked and cooled
> ¼ teaspoon cream of tartar
> ¼ cup confectioners' sugar
> ½ cup slivered almonds

Heat the oven to 350 degrees.

Lightly beat the egg yolks. Combine them with the applesauce, brown sugar, lemon rind and salt in a saucepan. Cook over moderate heat, stirring constantly, until the mixture is the consistency of custard. Pour the custard into the cooled pastry shell.

Beat the egg whites in a small bowl until they are foamy. Gradually add the cream of tartar and the confectioners' sugar and continue beating until a stiff meringue forms. Spread it over the pie filling and sprinkle with the almonds. Bake for 10 to 15 minutes, or until the meringue is a light golden brown.

Cool the pie completely or chill before serving.

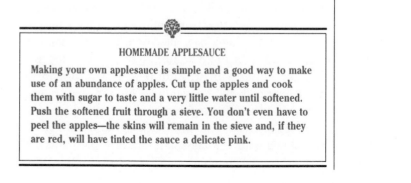

HOMEMADE APPLESAUCE

Making your own applesauce is simple and a good way to make use of an abundance of apples. Cut up the apples and cook them with sugar to taste and a very little water until softened. Push the softened fruit through a sieve. You don't even have to peel the apples—the skins will remain in the sieve and, if they are red, will have tinted the sauce a delicate pink.

Autumn Bavarian Pie

Serves 8

A satiny, luscious chocolate cream makes this a truly memorable dessert. For a touch of autumn, top the pie with spiced whipped cream. Chocolate leaves are a dramatic and appealing addition, but the pie tastes just as good without them.

> *1⅔ cups milk*
> *1 tablespoon (1 package) unflavored gelatin*
> *⅔ cup sugar*
> *⅓ cup unsweetened cocoa powder*
> *2 tablespoons (1 ounce) butter or margarine*
> *¾ teaspoon vanilla extract*
> *½ cup heavy cream*
> *9-inch baked pastry shell or crumb crust*
>
> SPICED WHIPPED CREAM:
> *½ cup heavy cream*
> *1 tablespoon sugar*
> *¼ teaspoon vanilla extract*
> *¼ teaspoon cinnamon*
> *⅛ teaspoon ground nutmeg*
>
> *Chocolate leaves (optional)*

Pour 1 cup of milk into a saucepan. Sprinkle the gelatin over the milk and let stand for 2 minutes.

Combine the sugar with the cocoa and stir into the milk mixture. Cook over moderate heat, stirring constantly, until the mixture boils. Remove from the heat, add the butter and stir until it is melted. Stir in the remaining milk and the vanilla. Chill the mixture until it begins to set, stirring occasionally.

Beat the cream until stiff peaks form. Carefully fold the cream into the chocolate mixture until blended.

Pour the chocolate filling into the pie shell and chill until set.

Prepare the spiced whipped cream just before serving the pie. Combine all the ingredients in a chilled bowl and beat until stiff.

Decorate the pie with the spiced whipped cream and, if desired, chocolate leaves.

CHOCOLATE LEAVES

> *½ cup semisweet chocolate chips*
> *6–8 stemmed leaves, such as rose, lemon or grape ivy, washed and dried*

You can make the leaves a few hours in advance and chill them until needed.

Melt the chocolate chips in the top of a double boiler over hot, not boiling, water. Remove from the heat and keep the pan over warm water.

Using a small pastry brush, spread a thin layer of melted chocolate on the underside of each leaf.

Set the leaves, chocolate side up, on a tray covered with wax paper and let them sit until the chocolate is firm. Carefully peel each leaf away from the chocolate leaf. Store the chocolate leaves, covered, in a cool place until ready to use.

CHAPTER 3

CAKES AND CHEESECAKES

S peed is not the only plus when you bake a cake in the microwave. A microwaved cake is light, fluffy, tender and moist. Using a microwave saves energy, too, because there is no need to preheat the oven and the baking time is shorter. However, do not be surprised by the appearance of the cake when you take it from the microwave. It will not be browned and may look under-cooked, even though it is not.

Some cakes will always bake better in a conventional oven—the longer cooking time allows the flavor of certain ingredients to develop and also leaves the outside of the cake pleasantly brown, which is important if you are not planning to frost it.

Whichever method of baking you decide to use, always check for doneness rather than relying solely on time. A toothpick or cake tester inserted in the center of the cake should come out clean, and the cake should begin to pull away from the sides of the pan when it is ready to come out of the oven.

Brandied Apricot Torte

Serves 6 to 8

Here is one way to dress up a store-bought pound cake and turn it into a really special dessert.

1 frozen loaf (10¾ ounces) pound cake
1 cup apricot preserves
2 tablespoons brandy or apricot brandy
2 tablespoons (1 ounce) butter
1 tablespoon light corn syrup
2 ounces semisweet chocolate
Fresh or canned apricots, sliced

Trim the top and side crusts from the pound cake. Slice the cake horizontally into 3 layers.

Put the apricot preserves in a 1-quart glass measure, cover and microwave on High (100 percent) for 1½ to 2 minutes, until hot and bubbly. Press the preserves through a strainer into a small bowl. Discard the pulp. Add 1 tablespoon of brandy to the strained preserves.

Set the bottom layer of the cake on a wire rack and spread with 2 tablespoons of the preserves. Top with the second layer and spread with another 2 tablespoons of preserves. Cover with the third cake layer. Spread the top and sides of the cake with the remaining preserves. Chill the cake for at least 1 hour.

To make the frosting, put the butter in a 1-quart glass measure with the remaining tablespoon of brandy and the corn syrup. Cover and microwave on High (100 percent) for 1 to 1½ minutes, until the butter is melted and the mixture is bubbling. Add the chocolate and stir until it is melted. Cool the frosting to lukewarm.

Frost the top and sides of the chilled cake and return to the refrigerator for about 30 minutes to firm up the frosting. Decorate the cake with apricot slices.

Walnut Cake

Serves 8 to 10

For the freshest nuts, buy them at a store where they are sold loose and in bulk rather than prepackaged. Natural food and gourmet shops are usually good sources.

The nuts and sour cream make this cake so rich and moist that a dusting of confectioners' sugar is all it needs. If you want to serve it frosted, try it with the Meringue Buttercream on page 42.

> *12 tablespoons (6 ounces) butter, softened*
> *¾ cup packed brown sugar*
> *3 large eggs, separated*
> *2 cups all-purpose flour*
> *1 teaspoon baking soda*
> *¼ teaspoon salt*
> *1 cup crushed, chopped walnuts*
> *1 teaspoon vanilla extract*
> *¾ cup sour cream*
> *¼ cup granulated sugar*

Heat the oven to 350 degrees. Butter a 9-by-5-inch loaf pan.

Cream the butter until light and smooth. Add the brown sugar and continue to beat until the mixture is fluffy. Beat in the egg yolks one at a time. After the last one is incorporated, continue to beat the batter for another minute or two.

Sift together the flour, baking soda and salt.

Toss ½ cup of the flour mixture with the crushed nuts. Stir the nuts and vanilla into the sour cream.

Gradually combine the remaining flour mixture and the sour cream mixture with the batter in alternating additions.

Beat the egg whites in a small bowl until frothy. Add the granulated sugar and continue to beat until stiff peaks form.

Stir about a third of the egg whites into the batter, then fold in the rest. Do not overmix.

Spoon the batter into the prepared pan and bake for 45 to 55 minutes, until a toothpick inserted in the middle of the cake comes out clean.

Cool the cake in the pan for about 10 minutes and then turn it out onto a wire rack to cool completely.

Blueberry Coffeecake

Serves 6 to 8

Try this during the summer when fresh blueberries are in season—and enjoy it at a leisurely breakfast or with an afternoon glass of iced tea.

> *4 tablespoons (2 ounces) butter*
> *¾ cup sugar*
> *1 large egg*
> *1½ cups all-purpose flour*
> *1 teaspoon baking powder*
> *½ teaspoon ground nutmeg*
> *½ cup milk*
> *1 cup fresh or frozen blueberries*

Beat the butter with the sugar and the egg until the mixture is light and fluffy.

Sift together the flour, baking powder and nutmeg.

Gradually stir the dry ingredients into the butter mixture, alternating with the milk. Gently fold in the blueberries.

Lightly butter and flour a 9-inch-square glass pan. Spread the batter in the pan and microwave on High (100 percent) for 4 minutes, rotating the pan a quarter turn after 2 minutes. Let the cake stand for 10 to 15 minutes before serving.

It is important to let the coffeecake stand for at least 10 minutes after taking it from the microwave.

Pumpkin Cake

Serves 8 to 10

A dense, moist bundt cake enhanced by a sprinkling of a crunchy brown sugar mixture. Serve it with morning coffee without topping, or with topping as a dessert.

¾ cup brown sugar, firmly packed
1 tablespoon cinnamon
¾ cup chopped walnuts
18½-ounce package yellow cake mix
4 large eggs
2 cups pumpkin puree
½ cup mayonnaise
¼ cup milk
2 teaspoons pumpkin pie spice
1 teaspoon vanilla extract
1 cup heavy cream
Walnut halves, for decoration

As most regular bundt pans are metal, you will need to buy one specially designed for use in the microwave.

Combine the brown sugar, cinnamon and walnuts.

Put the cake mix in a large bowl. Add the eggs, 1 cup of the pumpkin puree, the mayonnaise, milk, pumpkin pie spice and vanilla and mix until well combined. Pour half the batter into a buttered 3-quart microwavable bundt cake pan. Sprinkle with half the brown sugar mixture and then pour in the remaining batter.

Microwave on Medium (50 percent) for 20 minutes, rotating the pan a half turn after 10 minutes. Let the cake stand for 9 minutes, still in the pan, then turn it out onto a serving platter and cool completely.

About 30 minutes before serving, whip the cream in a chilled bowl until very stiff. Do not overbeat. Combine the remaining cup of pumpkin with the remaining sugar mixture. Fold this into the whipped cream and chill the mixture until you are ready to serve.

Just before serving, spread the chilled topping over the top of the cake and decorate with walnut halves.

Swirl Cake

Serves 8 to 10

Honey and nuts enliven this chocolate-swirled cake.

> *1 cup (8 ounces) butter*
> *2 cups sugar*
> *1 teaspoon vanilla extract*
> *5 large eggs*
> *2½ cups all-purpose flour*
> *¾ teaspoon baking soda*
> *¼ teaspoon salt*
> *1½ cups sour cream*
> *8-ounce milk chocolate bar, broken into pieces*
> *½ cup chocolate syrup*
> *¼ cup honey or light corn syrup*
> *¾ cup chopped pecans*
> *Confectioners' sugar (optional)*

Beat the butter with the sugar and vanilla until the mixture is light and fluffy. Add the eggs and beat well.

Combine the flour, baking soda and salt and gradually add them to the butter mixture, alternating with the sour cream.

Put the chocolate pieces and the chocolate syrup in a glass bowl. Microwave on High (100 percent) for 1 to 2 minutes, just until the chocolate pieces are melted.

Measure out 2 cups of batter and stir in the honey or corn syrup and the nuts. Stir the melted chocolate into the remaining batter.

Turn the chocolate batter into a buttered 3-quart microwavable bundt pan. Spoon the light batter evenly over the chocolate. Microwave on High (100 percent) for 20 to 25 minutes, until the cake tests done, rotating the pan a quarter turn every 5 minutes.

Cool the cake in the pan for 30 minutes, then remove it from the pan and cool completely on a wire rack. Sprinkle with confectioners' sugar or frost as desired.

Pina Colada Cheesecake with Pineapple Glaze

Serves 10

Pineapple, coconut milk and a touch of rum—the tastes of the South Seas—are present in every bite of this rich cheesecake. Lining the pan with overlapping sheets of transparent wrap is a handy technique that makes it easy to lift the chilled cake from the pan.

1 cup vanilla wafer crumbs
½ cup shredded coconut
3 tablespoons (1½ ounces) butter, melted
8-ounce can crushed pineapple
18 ounces cream cheese, softened
½ cup plus 2 tablespoons sugar
3 tablespoons all-purpose flour
2 large eggs
1 large egg yolk
2 tablespoons canned cream of coconut
2 tablespoons rum
1 tablespoon cornstarch

Combine the wafer crumbs, coconut and butter in a bowl and mix well.

Line the bottom and sides of an 8-inch round glass cake pan with 2 pieces of transparent wrap so that they overlap by 1 inch in the center of the dish and overhang the sides slightly. Press the crumb mixture firmly and evenly over the bottom of the pan and chill until firm.

Drain 3 tablespoons of juice from the pineapple and reserve. Put the remaining juice and the pineapple in a 2-cup glass measure, cover, and set aside.

Combine the cream cheese, ½ cup of sugar and the flour in a large microwavable bowl and beat until well blended. Add the eggs one at a time and the egg yolk.

Stir in the reserved pineapple juice, the cream of coconut and the rum.

Microwave the batter on High (100 percent) for 5 to 6 minutes, stirring every minute, until very hot. It will be lumpy.

Pour the batter into the chilled crust and smooth the top. Microwave on Medium (50 percent) for 6 to 8 minutes, rotating the dish a quarter turn every 2 minutes, until the center is almost set. Cool at room temperature and then chill thoroughly in the refrigerator.

To make the glaze, drain the juice from the reserved pineapple and mix it with the cornstarch, stirring until smooth. Add the remaining 2 tablespoons sugar, then stir the cornstarch mixture into the pineapple. Microwave on High (100 percent) for 2 to 3 minutes, stirring after 1½ minutes, until the glaze boils and thickens. Let it cool to room temperature.

To remove the cheesecake from the dish, take hold of the overlapping edges of the transparent wrap and lift up gently, supporting the cake underneath with your fingers. Set the cake on a serving platter and gently pull the transparent wrap out from beneath it.

Spread the pineapple glaze over the cheesecake and chill for at least 4 hours before serving.

CHEESECAKES: TRADITIONAL/NONTRADITIONAL?

Traditional cheesecakes, which require long, slow cooking and very slow cooling (to prevent drying and cracking), generally do better in conventional rather than microwave ovens. However, less traditional versions, such as the Pina Colada Cheesecake, do just fine in the microwave.

Almond-Chocolate Cheesecake

Serves 10 to 12

Chocolate-flavored cheesecake with a topping of milk chocolate and toasted almonds—who needs more?

Blanch almonds by microwaving 1 cup of water until boiling. Add the nuts and microwave on High (100 percent) for about 30 seconds. The skins will slip off easily.

1 tablespoon butter
¼ cup vanilla wafer, cake or graham cracker crumbs
2 8-ounce packages cream cheese, softened
2 cups chocolate milk
4 large eggs
½ teaspoon vanilla extract
1 cup plus 1 tablespoon sugar
⅓ cup cornstarch
½ teaspoon salt
½ cup sliced almonds
1 cup sour cream
3⅞-ounce bar milk chocolate, finely chopped

Heat the oven to 350 degrees. Butter a 9-inch springform pan. Press the crumbs evenly into the pan and arrange a foil collar around it (see page 53).

Beat the cream cheese with the chocolate milk, eggs and vanilla until well blended. Mix 1 cup of sugar with the cornstarch and salt and stir into the cheese mixture.

Spoon the cheese mixture into the pan and smooth the top. Bake for 1½ hours, or until set in the center. Cool the cheesecake in the pan for about 1 hour.

While the cheesecake is cooling, spread the almonds in a shallow pan and put them in the same oven for 12 to 15 minutes, until toasted.

Stir the remaining tablespoon of sugar into the sour cream and spread the mixture over the cooled cheesecake. Sprinkle the almonds and chopped chocolate over the cheesecake. Chill the cake before serving.

CHAPTER 4

FILLINGS AND FROSTINGS

To most people, a cake is incomplete without frosting. Whether the cake is robed in a sweet, billowing buttercream or a shining glaze, the icing makes it pretty.

Frostings and fillings add texture and flavor to a cake and they should complement but never overwhelm it. If the cake is flavored with orange or lemon, try an orange or lemon frosting. Chocolate cake and chocolate frosting are a popular combination, yet some folks prefer the gentler marriage of yellow cake and chocolate frosting or chocolate cake and vanilla frosting. Mousses and custards make tasty fillings—providing rich, creamy and often unexpected flavor and texture.

Varying fillings and frostings gives the cake baker not only an opportunity for creativity and originality, but also the chance to have fun.

Classic Sugar Glaze

Makes about 1 1/2 cups

This icing, which is very easy to apply, gives fruitcakes, nut breads, tea cakes and small pastries a smooth, finished look.

>   *2 cups confectioners' sugar, sifted*
>   *3 tablespoons warm water*
>
>   FLAVORING (choose one of the following):
>   *Chocolate: Sift 1/4 cup unsweetened cocoa powder*
>   *with the confectioners' sugar*
>   *Orange: Substitute 2 tablespoons concentrated*
>   *orange juice for 2 tablespoons of the water*
>   *Lemon or lime: Substitute 1 tablespoon lemon*
>   *or lime juice for 1 tablespoon of the water*
>   *and color appropriately, if desired*
>   *Almond or vanilla: Stir in 1/2 teaspoon almond*
>   *or vanilla extract*
>   *Coffee: Substitute 2 tablespoons triple-strength*
>   *coffee for 2 tablespoons of the water*

Sift the confectioners' sugar into a mixing bowl and gradually stir in the water and flavoring. Beat until smooth.

FROSTING TIPS

One of the best ways to frost a cake is to chill it between each application of frosting. This gives the first layer of frosting (which is referred to as the "sealing coat") time to firm up so that the next, and usually final, layer is easy to apply and does not pick up any stray crumbs. Always wipe the cake spatula clean every time you lift it off the cake.

Classic Buttercream

Makes 3 cups

This deliciously rich, smooth frosting is a favorite with most people. It is also very versatile in both application and flavoring. Buttercream is ideal for piping roses and decorative borders on cakes. Bear in mind that it is sensitive to temperature and should be used at or near room temperature. It can be stored for at least a week in the refrigerator.

Never fill a pastry bag more than two-thirds full—a partially filled bag is much easier to control than a full bag. Buttercream roses and leaves can be piped onto wax paper and frozen. Simply take them from the freezer and position them on the cake an hour or so before serving.

> *12 tablespoons (6 ounces) unsalted butter, slightly softened*
> *4 cups confectioners' sugar, sifted*
> *2 tablespoons milk, cream or water*
> *1 teaspoon vanilla extract*

Put the butter in a mixing bowl, add half the sugar and beat until smooth and light. Beat in the remaining sugar, the liquid and the vanilla and continue beating until smooth.

VARIATIONS

> *Extra-rich: Beat in 1 large egg*
> *Chocolate: Substitute 2 ounces melted semi-sweet chocolate for the milk*
> *Coffee: Substitute 1 teaspoon instant espresso coffee dissolved in 1 tablespoon boiling water for 1 tablespoon of the milk*
> *Almond: Add ½ teaspoon almond extract*
> *Orange: Substitute equal quantities of strong, orange juice or Grand Marnier for the milk*

Meringue Buttercream

Makes about 2 cups

Keep this frosting at room temperature (65 to 75 degrees) while you are spreading it on a cake or piping it from a bag. The buttercream can be stored in the refrigerator, but always allow it to come to room temperature before working with it.

> *2 large egg whites*
> *1 cup confectioners' sugar, sifted*
> *8 tablespoons (4 ounces) unsalted butter, softened*
>
> FLAVORING (optional; choose one of the
>   following):
> *1 teaspoon vanilla or lemon extract*
> *1 tablespoon Grand Marnier or Cointreau*
> *2 ounces semisweet chocolate, melted*
> *1 tablespoon raspberry syrup*
> *1 teaspoon instant espresso coffee dissolved
>   in 1 tablespoon water*

For the most luxurious finish, apply 3 coats of buttercream frosting and smooth the final layer with a cake spatula that has been dipped in hot water and then wiped dry.

Combine the egg whites and the confectioners' sugar in a bowl over simmering water, stirring until the mixture is smooth and tepid. Do not allow it to get hot. Remove it from the heat and allow to cool slightly, then beat until stiff peaks form.

Whip the butter until soft and smooth. Beat it, a tablespoon at a time, into the stiffened egg whites. Continue beating until smooth; you may have to beat the frosting for 4 or 5 minutes with an electric beater to reach the proper consistency.

If you are flavoring the buttercream, beat the flavoring in last.

Cream Cheese Buttercream

Makes about 3½ cups

The cream cheese gives this icing a hint of tartness and marvelous texture.

Use a sturdy
standing electric
mixer to make
buttercream, if
possible.

> *8 tablespoons (4 ounces) unsalted butter, softened*
> *8 ounces cream cheese, softened*
> *2¾ cups confectioners' sugar, sifted*
> *2 teaspoons milk or vanilla extract*

Beat the butter with the cream cheese until the mixture is fluffy. Gradually add the confectioners' sugar and the milk or extract and continue beating until smooth and light.

Chocolate Frosting

Makes about 1 cup

A chocolate frosting dresses up the simplest yellow cake or brownie. With a microwave, this version is incredibly easy.

> *½ cup semisweet chocolate chips*
> *2 tablespoons vegetable shortening*
> *2 tablespoons milk*
> *½ cup confectioners' sugar*

Combine the chocolate chips, shortening and milk in a 1-quart glass measure. Microwave on High (100 percent) for 30 to 40 seconds until melted.

Add the confectioners' sugar and whisk until the mixture is smooth.

Chocolate Marshmallow Glaze

Makes 1 cup

Semisweet chocolate and marshmallow cream combine to make a smooth glaze to pour over a plain butter cake, a dense chocolate cake or spread on large sugar cookies.

> *⅓ cup sugar*
> *3 tablespoons water*
> *1 cup semisweet chocolate chips*
> *3 tablespoons marshmallow cream*

Combine the sugar and the water in a small microwavable mixing bowl. Microwave on High (100 percent) for 1 minute or until boiling.

Immediately add the chocolate chips and stir until melted. Add the marshmallow cream and stir until well blended. If you prefer a thinner glaze, stir in hot water, ¼ teaspoon at a time.

Cocoa Fudge Frosting

Makes 2 cups

Frostings that use confectioners' sugar as their base are quick to make, easy to spread and deliciously sweet.

> *4 tablespoons (4 ounces) butter*
> *½ cup unsweetened cocoa powder*
> *2⅔ cups (1-pound package) confectioners' sugar*
> *⅓ cup milk*
> *1 teaspoon vanilla extract*

Put the butter in a glass mixing bowl and microwave on High (100 percent) for 1 minute or until melted.

Add the cocoa to the melted butter and stir until smooth. Microwave on High (100 percent) for 30 seconds to 1 minute, until the mixture boils.

Add the confectioners' sugar and the milk. Beat with an electric mixer until the frosting is of spreading consistency. Stir in the vanilla.

Chocolate Mousse Filling

Makes 3 cups

For a chocolate lover—and there are many of us—the only thing better than chocolate cake or chocolate mousse is a combination of the two. A creamy chocolate mousse makes a light and altogether irresistible filling for any cake, chocolate or otherwise.

> *1 tablespoon (1 package) unflavored gelatin*
> *2 tablespoons cold water*
> *⅓ cup water*
> *⅓ cup unsweetened cocoa powder*
> *⅔ cup sugar*
> *1½ cups heavy cream*
> *2 teaspoons vanilla extract*

Sprinkle the gelatin over the 2 tablespoons of cold water in a small bowl and let it soften for 2 to 3 minutes.

Bring ⅓ cup of water to the boil in a small saucepan. Reduce the heat and stir in the cocoa. When the mixture is smooth and thickened, add the softened gelatin and stir until completely dissolved. Remove from the heat and stir in the sugar. Let the mixture cool to room temperature.

Beat together the cream and the vanilla until stiff peaks form. With the beater on low speed, gradually add the the chocolate mixture, beating just until blended. Chill the mousse for 30 minutes before using.

CHAPTER 5

PUDDINGS, CUSTARDS AND MOUSSES

Puddings and custards have a universal appeal. Stirred or baked, served warm, cold or frozen, their smoothness and silkiness make them satisfying and soothing. They are as seasonless as they are ageless, equally inviting on a cold wintry night as on a warm summer evening.

Custards, which are thickened with eggs, traditionally are stirred on top of the stove over low heat so that the eggs will not curdle. The microwave takes all worry out of making these fragile desserts—it cooks them gently and swiftly, leaving them with a perfect, delicate texture.

Serve a pudding or custard after a sophisticated dinner party or a simple supper. On either occasion, the dessert will be just right—puddings, custards and mousses always are.

Rice Pudding

Serves 6

When you use a microwave and this quick, delicious recipe, you can have rice pudding for dinner again, and again, and again.

> 1 cup water
> ½ teaspoon salt
> 1 cup uncooked instant rice
> ½ cup sugar
> 1 tablespoon cornstarch
> 2½ cups milk
> 2 large eggs, lightly beaten
> ½ cup raisins
> ¼ teaspoon ground nutmeg

Put the water and salt in a 1½-quart microwavable casserole and microwave on High (100 percent) for 3 to 4 minutes, until boiling. Stir in the rice and allow to stand for 5 minutes until the water is absorbed.

Mix the sugar with the cornstarch in a large bowl. Add the milk and eggs and stir until smooth.

Add the mixture to the rice in the casserole and stir to combine. Stir in the raisins and half the nutmeg. Microwave on High (100 percent) for 8 to 10 minutes, stirring every 2 minutes, until the pudding is creamy and thickened.

Sprinkle the remaining nutmeg over the top. Cover the pudding with transparent wrap and allow it to cool. Serve it at room temperature or chilled.

Egg-based puddings will keep in the refrigerator for 4 to 5 days.

Individual Coffee-Caramel Flans

Serves 4

Watch custards carefully as they cook. Overcooking tends to toughen them, even in the microwave.

Nothing is as soothing and satisfying as caramel-topped custard. Making individual serving-sized flans in the microwave is nearly foolproof.

> ½ cup sugar
> 3 large eggs
> 2 large egg yolks
> ¼ cup coffee liqueur
> 3 tablespoons sugar
> 1 teaspoon vanilla extract
> ⅛ teaspoon salt
> 2 cups half-and-half

Sprinkle the sugar evenly over the bottom of a 10-inch skillet and set over low heat until the sugar melts to a light golden syrup, stirring occasionally with a wooden spoon.

Pour the syrup into 4 8-ounce glass custard cups. Tilt the cups to coat the bottoms and halfway up the sides. Allow the syrup to cool and harden.

Put the eggs, egg yolks, liqueur, sugar, vanilla and salt in a large bowl and stir to combine.

Pour the half-and-half into a 2-cup glass measure and scald by microwaving on High (100 percent) for 2½ to 3 minutes. Do not allow the liquid to boil. Slowly whisk the half-and-half into the egg mixture. Divide the mixture equally among the custard cups.

Arrange the cups in a circle in the microwave. Microwave on Medium (50 percent) for 4½ to 6 minutes, turning the cups every 2 minutes, until a knife inserted near the outer edge comes out clean. The center will set while the custards are cooling. Chill the custard thoroughly before serving.

To serve, loosen each custard around the edge with a knife. Invert a dessert plate over the cup. Holding the cup and plate together, quickly turn them over and shake gently so that the custard is released. Repeat with the remaining custards.

Bread Pudding

Serves 4

Served with the Hot Buttered Rum-Raisin Sauce on page 77, this bread pudding becomes a sophisticated dessert.

> 2 tablespoons butter
> 2 eggs
> 1 cup milk
> ⅓ cup sugar
> ¼ cup raisins
> 1 teaspoon vanilla extract
> ⅛ teaspoon salt
> 1½ cups cubed day-old bread

Melt the butter in a 1-quart microwavable casserole. Add the eggs and beat well.

Stir the milk, sugar, raisins, vanilla and salt into the eggs. Add the bread cubes, toss to cover completely and let the mixture stand for 5 minutes. Stir it gently from time to time to insure that the bread cubes absorb the liquid.

Microwave on High, uncovered, for 5 to 6 minutes, until set. Stir the pudding once, after 3 minutes.

Chocolate Pudding

Serves 4

With a microwave, you can make *real* chocolate pudding almost instantly. You can eat it hot, if you like, too.

> ⅔ *cup sugar*
> ¼ *cup unsweetened cocoa powder*
> 3 *tablespoons cornstarch*
> ¼ *teaspoon salt*
> 2¼ *cups milk*
> 2 *tablespoons butter*
> 1 *teaspoon vanilla extract*

Combine the sugar, cocoa, cornstarch and salt in a microwavable glass bowl. Gradually stir in the milk until the mixture is smooth.

Microwave on High (100 percent) for 4 to 6 minutes, stirring after 2 or 3 minutes. Microwave on High for another 1 to 2 minutes, or until the pudding is thickened. Stir in the butter and vanilla.

Pour the pudding into individual dessert dishes or a serving bowl. Cover with transparent wrap and chill until ready to serve.

Transparent wrap set directly on top of pudding as it chills will prevent a skin from forming.

Fresh Peach Yogurt Mousse

Serves 8

Juicy fresh peaches combine with plain yogurt to make a light-as-air frozen dessert.

> *6-ounce package gelatin*
> *1½ cups boiling water*
> *⅓ cup lemon juice*
> *2 large egg whites*
> *⅓ cup sugar*
> *¼ teaspoon salt*
> *1 cup plain yogurt*
> *1 large, fresh, ripe peach, finely chopped*
> *(about 1 cup)*
> *Peach slices, for decoration*

Combine the gelatin with the boiling water and stir to dissolve the gelatin. Stir in the lemon juice and chill until the mixture begins to set.

Beat the egg whites until foamy. Gradually add the sugar and salt and beat until stiff peaks form.

Fold the yogurt and 1 cup of the partially set gelatin into the egg whites.

Add the chopped peaches to the rest of the gelatin. Fold this mixture into the egg whites.

Turn the mousse into a 6-cup mold or 8 individual serving cups. Cover with transparent wrap and chill for 2 to 3 hours or until firm.

To serve, unmold the mousse and decorate with peach slices.

Mocha Frozen Cream

Serves 8

Rich, smooth frozen puddings are particularly welcomed by the cook because they can be made days in advance. Try inserting a popsicle stick into these when they are partially frozen and then freezing them completely—presto! Homemade pudding pops.

> *⅓ cup milk*
> *2 tablespoons instant coffee*
> *1 cup miniature marshmallows*
> *½ cup semisweet chocolate chips*
> *¼ cup chopped almonds*
> *1 tablespoon brandy (optional)*
> *1½ cups whipped cream*

Combine the milk with the instant coffee in a microwavable glass bowl. Stir in the marshmallows and chocolate chips. Microwave on High (100 percent) for 1 to 2 minutes, until the mixture is just coming to the boil. Remove from the microwave and stir until smooth. Stir in the almonds and brandy and let cool.

Gently fold the whipped cream into the chocolate mixture. Spoon the pudding into 8 paper-lined muffin cups. Cover and freeze until firm. Serve with additional whipped cream, if desired.

Frozen Lemon Mousse

Serves 6

Serve this refreshing summer dessert with Raspberry Sauce (see page 74).

1½ teaspoons (½ package) unflavored gelatin
½ cup lemon juice
3 large eggs, separated
½ cup sugar
3 tablespoon grated lemon rind
⅛ teaspoon salt
1 cup heavy cream
2 vanilla wafers, crumbled

Fit a 1-quart soufflé dish with a 2-inch collar of aluminum foil.

Combine the gelatin with the lemon juice in a 1-cup glass measure. Microwave on Medium (50 percent) for 40 to 60 seconds until the gelatin is dissolved.

Beat the egg yolks and ¼ cup sugar until smooth and lemony yellow. Fold in the gelatin mixture and the lemon rind.

Put the egg whites and salt in a large bowl, and beat with an electric mixer until foamy. Gradually add the remaining sugar and beat until stiff peaks form.

Beat the cream with an electric mixer until stiff. Gently fold the beaten egg whites and the cream into the egg mixture, being careful not to overblend—some white may show.

Pour the mixture into the prepared soufflé dish and sprinkle the top with the wafer crumbs. Freeze the mousse for several hours or overnight.

To make a foil collar on a soufflé dish, wrap a strip of foil about 3 inches wide around the dish so that it extends above the rim. Secure it with kitchen twine or tape.

CHAPTER 6

CANDIES AND SWEET SNACKS

C andy helps us celebrate holidays and birthdays; it also helps us through dark times and tired days; it serves as reward for a task well done and a treat after a grueling exercise. Children adore it, adults try to resist it (rarely successfully!), everyone craves it once in a while. Here are some recipes for satisfying these cravings—with *some* moderation!

Easy Chocolate Chip Fudge

Makes 16 2-inch squares

The easiest fudge recipe going—and one of the best.

> 1 ⅓ *cups sweetened condensed milk*
> 2 *cups semisweet chocolate chips*
> ½ *cup chopped nuts (optional)*
> 1 *teaspoon vanilla extract*

Combine the condensed milk and chocolate chips in a mixing bowl. Microwave on High (100 percent) for 1 to 1½ minutes, until the mixture is smooth when stirred.

Stir in the chopped nuts, if desired, and the vanilla. Spread the mixture in a buttered 8-inch square pan. Cover lightly with transparent wrap and chill until firm. Cut into 2-inch squares and serve.

Fudge Candy

Makes 81 1-inch squares

This variation of classic fudge is so simple to make that even young children can manage it. The addition of marshmallow cream makes it especially sweet and smooth—just the way kids like it.

> 5-ounce can evaporated milk
> 2¼ cups sugar
> ½ teaspoon salt
> 6-ounce package semisweet chocolate chips
> 8-ounce bar milk chocolate, broken in pieces
> 7-ounce jar marshmallow cream
> ½ teaspoon vanilla extract

Combine the milk, sugar and salt in a 4-quart microwavable casserole. Microwave on High (100 percent) for 3 minutes, stirring after 2 minutes. Microwave on High (100 percent) for 4 to 5 minutes longer.

Add the chocolate chips, milk chocolate and marshmallow cream and stir until the ingredients are thoroughly blended. Stir in the vanilla.

Pour the mixture into a buttered 9-inch-square pan. Cool thoroughly. When the fudge is completely cold, cut it into 1-inch squares.

Chocolate chips do not *look* melted when they are heated in the microwave. Instead they appear softened and shiny but still in the shape of chips. Just stir them to smooth them out. Do not increase the time in the microwave.

Chocolate-Covered Grasshoppers

Serves 10

A sweetened candy version of the after-dinner cocktail.

16-ounce bag marshmallows
½ cup milk
1 cup semisweet chocolate chips
2 tablespoons vegetable shortening
3 tablespoons crème de menthe
3 tablespoons crème de cacao
1 cup heavy cream, whipped
4 ounces milk chocolate

When microwaving marshmallows, it is a good idea to mix them with liquid. A single marshmallow cooked too long in the microwave might explode.

Put the marshmallows and milk in a large microwavable bowl. Microwave on High (100 percent) for 3 to 4 minutes, stirring after 1½ minutes, until the marshmallows are puffy and melted. Whisk the mixture until smooth and cool to room temperature.

Combine the chocolate chips and the shortening in a 2-cup glass measure. Microwave on High (100 percent) for 35 to 45 seconds. Stir the mixture until it is smooth.

Divide the chocolate among 10 paper-lined custard cups. Using the back of a spoon, smooth the melted chocolate evenly over the bottom and sides of each paper lining. Chill until the chocolate is firm.

Whip the cream in a chilled bowl. Stir the crème de menthe and the crème de cacao into the cooled marshmallows. When thoroughly blended, fold in the whipped cream.

Carefully peel the paper off the chocolate cups. Fill each cup with the marshmallow mixture and chill for 2 to 3 hours.

Make shavings from the milk chocolate bar and sprinkle them over each filled cup before serving.

Toffee Squares

Makes about 3 dozen

These are a chewy cross between a bar and a candy.

> *1 cup sugar*
> *1 cup (8 ounces) butter, softened*
> *¼ teaspoon salt*
> *1 egg, separated*
> *1 tablespoon Amaretto liqueur*
> *2 teaspoons grated orange rind*
> *2 cups sifted all-purpose flour*
> *½ cup slivered almonds, coarsely chopped*

Heat the oven to 300 degrees.

Cream the sugar, butter and salt until fluffy. Add the egg yolk, Amaretto and orange rind and beat until smooth.

Gradually stir in the flour. (The dough will be stiff.) Spread the dough in an even layer over an ungreased baking sheet, patting it gently to make it flat.

Beat the egg white in a small bowl until foamy and paint it over the dough. Press the almonds into the top.

Bake for 40 to 45 minutes, until firm and lightly browned. Cut into squares while still warm.

Rocky Road Candy

Makes 81 1-inch squares

An old-time favorite made in the microwave.

> 2 8-ounce bars milk chocolate
> 3 cups miniature marshmallows
> ¾ cup toasted rice cereal
> ¼ cup shredded, sweetened coconut

Put the chocolate bars in a 2-quart glass measure. Microwave on High (100 percent) for 2 minutes, then and stir until smooth.

Stir in the marshmallows, cereal and coconut. Spread the mixture in a buttered 9-inch-square pan and chill until firm. When thoroughly chilled, cut the candy into 1-inch squares. Keep refrigerated.

Peanut Butter Chocolate Truffles

Makes about 32 truffles

Cocoa-dusted truffles are not difficult to make and will impress your guests every time. These are flavored with peanut butter; try them with pure chocolate, too.

> ⅔ cup heavy cream
> 10 ounces milk chocolate, broken into pieces
> ½ cup creamy peanut butter
> 1 teaspoon vanilla extract
> Cocoa, for dusting

Heat the cream in a saucepan until it is just about to boil. Put the chocolate pieces in a mixing bowl. Pour the hot cream over the chocolate and beat until the mixture is smooth.

Stir in the peanut butter and vanilla. Chill the mixture for about 2 hours, until firm.

Spread the cocoa on a plate or piece of wax paper. Roll the chilled chocolate mixture between the palms of your hands to form 1-inch balls. Roll the balls in the cocoa, shaking off any excess, so that they are evenly coated. Chill the truffles on a plate until ready to serve.

Nut Buttercrunch

Makes about 1 pound

When you set this nut candy out for a group, the crunchy shards will be gone in a twinkling.

> *½ cup chopped walnuts*
> *8 tablespoons (4 ounces) butter*
> *¾ cup packed brown sugar*
> *1 tablespoon light corn syrup*
> *1 cup semisweet chocolate chips*

Line an 8-inch-square pan with foil and lightly butter the foil. Sprinkle the nuts in the prepared pan.

Melt the butter in a saucepan and add the brown sugar and corn syrup. Bring to the boil over moderate heat, stirring constantly.

Reduce the heat and boil gently for 4 minutes, stirring occasionally. Quickly pour the mixture evenly over the nuts in the pan and let it cool slightly.

Sprinkle with the chocolate chips. Allow them to soften, then spread the chocolate evenly with a spatula. Chill the mixture until firm. Remove the buttercrunch from the pan and cut or break into pieces.

Glazed Raisinola

Makes about 7 cups

A delicious version of granola, this snack keeps best if stored in airtight containers in the refrigerator. But its storing potential is unlikely to be a problem; once your family tastes it, the granola will disappear in a matter of hours.

> *2 cups quick or old-fashioned rolled oats, uncooked*
> *1 cup shredded coconut*
> *½ cup wheat germ*
> *½ cup shelled sunflower seeds*
> *½ cup slivered almonds*
> *8 tablespoons (4 ounces) butter*
> *¼ cup honey*
> *½ teaspoon salt*
> *2 cups raisins*

Heat the oven to 300 degrees.

Combine the oats, coconut, wheat germ, sunflower seeds and almonds in a large bowl.

Put the butter, honey and salt in a small saucepan and heat, stirring, until well blended. Pour the butter mixture over the dry ingredients, mixing well. Spread the mixture in a buttered 15½-by-10½-inch jelly-roll pan.

Bake for 30 minutes, until golden brown, stirring several times during cooking. Remove from the oven and add the raisins while the mixture is still hot. Cool completely and serve, or store in airtight containers.

Deluxe Fruit Trail Mix

Makes about 3 cups

Monkeys drop coconuts from the tops of palm trees to crack the shells, but with this method of heating the whole coconut in the oven to facilitate removing the shell, tree climbing will be unnecessary. The flavor and texture of a fresh coconut is far better than canned coconut.

1 fresh coconut
8-ounces dried mixed fruits
½ cup pecans, shelled
2 tablespoons milk carob chips (optional)

Heat the oven to 350 degrees.

Puncture the eyes of the coconut and drain the liquid. Put the drained coconut in the oven for 20 minutes.

Remove the warm coconut from the oven and hit it with a hammer to remove the shell. Take off any remaining shell with a blunt knife.

Shred the coconut meat with a grater to make 1 cup. Reset the oven to 400 degrees.

Spread the shredded coconut on a baking sheet and toast for 2 to 5 minutes, stirring frequently until golden.

Combine the coconut in a bowl with the dried fruits, pecans and optional carob chips. Serve immediately or store in an airtight container.

Most candies store well in airtight containers such as plastic boxes and round tins with snug-fitting lids.

CHAPTER 7

FRUIT DESSERTS

It could be argued that, when a fruit is in season, the best way to enjoy it is to eat it fresh and uncooked, with no embellishments whatever. The first juicy peach of summer is truly a treat to be savored every year, as is the first sweet pear of autumn—but just imagine life without peach pie or poached pears! Fruit desserts are among the most loved of all, and in general taste best when made with fruits that are ripe and in season.

However, do not ignore dried and frozen fruit during those times of year when fresh fruit is not abundant. Raisins and other dried fruits, cherry pie filling and canned peach halves can be cooked into delicious and easy-to-prepare desserts that will give you and your family a lift on the most heavily clouded day. Whether you use fresh or preserved fruit, the dish you create is sure to be appreciated and quickly devoured. After all, who doesn't like fruit desserts?

Nectarine Country Shortcake

Serves 6

Serve this luscious old-style shortcake warm with homemade ice cream. Baking the nectarines with the shortcake makes the dessert soft-textured and moist.

Nectarines are in fact a variety of peach with a smooth skin and a distinct and lovely flavor—not a cross between a peach and a plum, as is sometimes believed. They are usually in season from June through August.

3 cups sliced fresh nectarines
6 tablespoons sugar
1½ cups sifted all-purpose flour
2 teaspoons baking powder
¼ teaspoon salt
¼ cup vegetable shortening
1 large egg, beaten
½ cup milk
½ cup packed brown sugar
½ teaspoon cinnamon
3 tablespoons (1½ ounces) butter, cut into pieces

Heat the oven to 425 degrees and butter a 9-inch-square pan.

Sprinkle the nectarines with 2 tablespoons of sugar and set aside.

Resift the flour with the remaining 4 tablespoons of sugar, the baking powder and salt. Add the shortening, rubbing it in with your fingertips until it resembles coarse crumbs.

Add the egg and milk all at once and stir to make a soft dough. Spread this in the prepared pan and cover with the sliced nectarines.

Combine the brown sugar, cinnamon and butter, working with your fingertips until the mixture is crumbly. Scatter the crumbs over the nectarines.

Bake for 25 minutes or until the shortcake is baked through in the center.

Lemonberry Saxon Pudding

Serves 6

This light lemony dessert looks and tastes particularly good served with a strawberry or raspberry sauce.

> *1 cup sugar*
> *¾ cup milk*
> *8 tablespoons (4 ounces) butter*
> *1 tablespoon grated lemon rind*
> *⅓ cup all-purpose flour*
> *⅓ cup cornstarch*
> *6 eggs, separated*
> *⅓ cup lemon juice*
> *⅛ teaspoon cream of tartar*
> *Strawberry Sauce (see page 74)*

Heat the oven to 350 degrees.

Butter 6 1½-cup ovenproof molds or bowls. Dust them with sugar and set aside.

Combine ½ cup of the sugar with the milk, butter and lemon rind in a saucepan and heat until the butter is melted.

Combine the flour and cornstarch in a bowl and stir into the hot milk mixture.

Pour the mixture into a blender or food processor fitted with a metal blade. With the machine running, add the egg yolks, and then the lemon juice. Blend until smooth, then pour into a mixing bowl and set aside.

Beat the egg whites with the cream of tartar until foamy. Gradually add the remaining sugar until soft peaks form. Fold the egg whites gently into the egg yolk and lemon mixture. Do not overmix.

Spoon equal amounts of the mixture into the prepared molds. Set the molds in a large pan and pour in hot water to a depth of 1 inch. Bake for 25 to 30 minutes, until set and lightly browned.

Remove the molds from the water bath and cool for 5 minutes. Loosen them around the edges with a knife and invert each one in turn onto a serving plate. Serve warm or chilled, in a pool of strawberry sauce.

Cherry Crisp

Serves 6 to 8

A crispy-topped pudding-like dessert that is fast and easy to make.

> 21-ounce can cherry pie filling
> 2 teaspoons lemon juice
> 2 teaspoons grated lemon rind
> 3 tablespoons (2 ounces) butter
> ¼ cup packed brown sugar
> ⅓ cup quick-cooking rolled oats
> ⅓ cup all-purpose flour
> 2 tablespoons chopped nuts

Combine the pie filling, lemon juice, and lemon rind in an 8-inch microwavable cake pan or round glass dish.

Put the butter in a microwavable bowl and microwave on High (100 percent) for 30 to 45 seconds until melted. Stir in the sugar and the oats. Microwave on High (100 percent) for 1 to 2 minutes until the mixture is hot and bubbly. Stir in the flour and nuts until the mixture is crumbly.

Sprinkle the crumbs over the cherry mixture in the cake pan. Microwave on High (100 percent) for 6 to 8 minutes until bubbly. Serve the dessert warm or cold.

Pears au Chocolat

Serves 6

Poached pears drizzled with chocolate sauce and crowned with whipped cream are an elegant ending to a fine meal. The pears are poached hours before serving. So that they hold their shape, allow them to cool in the poaching syrup.

> *6 fresh, medium-size pears*
> *¾ cup sugar*
> *1¼ cups water*
> *1½ teaspoons vanilla extract*
> *8 tablespoons finely chopped nuts*
> *3 tablespoons confectioners' sugar*
> *1½ teaspoons milk*
> *Creamy Chocolate Sauce (see page 72)*
> *Whipped cream (optional)*

For poaching, choose pears that are firm but have just a hint of surface softness.

Core the pears from the bottom end, leaving the stems intact. Peel them carefully and slice a small amount from the bottom of each to make a flat base.

Combine the sugar and water in a saucepan and add the pears. Cover the pan, bring the water to a gentle simmer and poach over low heat for 15 to 20 minutes, depending on the ripeness of the pears. Remove from the heat, add the vanilla and cool the pears in the syrup. Chill.

Combine the chopped nuts with the confectioners' sugar and milk in a small bowl until the mixture holds together. Spoon the nut mixture into the cored-out cavities in the pears and arrange them in a serving dish. Serve with chocolate sauce and whipped cream.

Peach Pie

Serves 6 to 8

This chilled peach pie will bring the taste of summer to the table at any time of year.

1 cup vanilla wafer crumbs
⅓ cup gingersnap crumbs
4 tablespoons (2 ounces) melted butter
2 28-ounce cans peach halves in heavy syrup
3 tablespoons cornstarch
3-ounce package cream cheese

Stir together the cookie crumbs and melted butter. Press the mixture into a 9½-inch microwavable pie plate or glass dish. Microwave on High (100 percent) for 1½ to 2 minutes, turning after 1 minute. Let the crust cool completely.

Drain the peaches, reserving the syrup. Put 3 peach halves in a blender or food processor and process until pureed. Add sufficient syrup to the puree to measure 1½ cups.

Combine the cornstarch and the puree in a 1-quart measure, whisking until smooth. Microwave on High (100 percent) for 4 minutes, whisking after 2 minutes.

Put the cream cheese in a 1-cup measure. Microwave on Medium (50 percent) for 45 seconds to soften. Spread the softened cream cheese over the bottom of the crumb crust.

Arrange as many of the remaining peach halves as will fit in the crust over the cream cheese, cut side down. Cut the rest of the halves into small pieces to fill the spaces.

Pour the hot peach puree over the peaches in the crust. Chill the pie for 2 to 3 hours before serving.

Nutmeg Lemon Cream

Serves 6

When you are in a hurry for something sweet and fruity, try this simple cream.

> *2 cups applesauce*
> *5⅓-ounce can sweetened evaporated milk*
> *⅔ cup apple juice*
> *½ teaspoon grated lemon rind*
> *¼ teaspoon ground nutmeg*
> *4-serving package instant lemon pudding*
> *Whipped cream (optional)*

Combine the applesauce, evaporated milk, apple juice, lemon rind and nutmeg in a mixing bowl.

Stir in the lemon pudding and beat with an electric mixer for about 1 minute, until smooth. Pour the mixture into individual dessert dishes or a serving bowl. Chill until thickened and serve with whipped cream.

Raisin Butterscotch Apples

Serves 4

Whole fruits hold their shape and keep their texture very well in the microwave. They cook best when arranged in a circle.

The microwave softens whole, cored apples in a few minutes. These are filled with sweet raisins and topped with brown sugar and butter.

> *4 medium-size apples*
> *¼ cup raisins*
> *3 tablespoons brown sugar*
> *¼ teaspoon ground nutmeg*
> *2 teaspoons butter*

Use a melon baller to remove the cores from the apples. Peel the top half of each apple.

Put the apples in a microwavable dish. Fill the cavities of each with 1 tablespoon of raisins.

Mix together the sugar and nutmeg and top the apples with equal amounts of this mixture. Finally, top each apple with ½ teaspoon of butter.

Cover the apples with transparent wrap. Microwave on High (100 percent) for 3 minutes, then turn a quarter turn and microwave for 3 to 4 minutes longer until the apples are tender.

Serve warm or at room temperature.

Blushing Apples

Serves 4 to 6

Here is a quick dessert that your family will love. The melted cinnamon candies give the apples a pinkish hue and the sour cream cuts the candies' sweetness.

> ¼ cup water
> ¼ cup sugar
> ½ cup tiny cinnamon candies
> 4 cups peeled, cored and sliced apples
> ½ cup sour cream

Combine the water, sugar and candies in a 1-quart glass measure. Microwave on High (100 percent) for 4 to 6 minutes, stirring twice until the candies are almost melted.

Add the apple slices to the melted candies and stir to coat them. Microwave on High (100 percent) for 1 minute. Spoon into serving dishes and let cool. Top each serving with a spoonful of sour cream.

Underripe fruit will not soften when cooked—even in the microwave. Leave it at room temperature for a few days to ripen completely before cooking.

Glazed Strawberry Pie

Serves 6 to 8

A colorful, pretty dessert that is a good choice for guests. It tastes wonderful and can be made hours ahead of serving.

9½-inch unbaked pie crust, in a glass pie dish
1½ quarts fresh strawberries
⅓ cup water
¾ cup sugar
2 ⅓ tablespoons cornstarch
⅛ teaspoon salt
Whipped cream, for decorating

Prick the pie crust with a fork and put it on an inverted microwavable dish in the microwave. Lay a sheet of paper towel on top of the crust. Microwave on High (100 percent) for 4 to 5 minutes, rotating a half turn after 2 minutes. Remove the pie dish from the microwave and let the crust cool.

Wash the strawberries and remove their stems. Crush 1 cup of the berries with a fork. Put the crushed strawberries in a 1-quart glass measure, add the water and microwave on High (100 percent) for 3 to 4 minutes until the berries are soft. Press the mixture through a strainer and add sufficient water to measure 1 cup.

Combine the sugar with the cornstarch and salt in a bowl. Gradually add the strained strawberry liquid, stirring until smooth. Return the mixture to the glass measure and microwave on High (100 percent) for 4 to 5 minutes, stirring after 2 minutes.

Spread the remaining strawberries over the bottom of the cooled pie crust. Pour the hot glaze evenly over the berries. Chill the pie for 2 to 3 hours and decorate with whipped cream before serving.

CHAPTER 8

SAUCES AND TOPPINGS

S auces and other toppings turn ordinary desserts into festive fare. Plain ice cream becomes a sundae with a spoonful of fudge sauce or raspberry sauce; lemon soufflé is made more elegant with strawberry sauce served on the side; pound cake tastes moister and richer with a generous helping of chocolate or fruit sauce.

Using a microwave to make sauces is easy and efficient. They take only minutes to cook and often can be stored and reheated (if necessary) in the same container. Make three or four different sauces and invite friends over for a make-your-own sundae party. With a little planning, you can always have several sauces on hand in the refrigerator and can relax and smile when unexpected guests—of any age—drop by.

Creamy Chocolate Sauce

Makes about 1 cup sauce

The sauce for Pears au Chocolat (see page 66) or any dessert that deserves it. Cook it on the stove top while the pears are poaching, or in the microwave, as you prefer.

> 6 tablespoons water
> 6 tablespoons sugar
> 4 tablespoons (2 ounces) butter
> 1 ⅓ cups semisweet chocolate chips

Combine the water, sugar and butter in a saucepan and bring to the full boil. Remove the pan from the heat and stir in the chocolate chips. Stir until the chocolate has melted completely. Beat or whisk the sauce until smooth. Cool.

Or, put all the ingredients in a 4-cup glass measure and microwave on High (100 percent) for 2 minutes. Stir, then microwave on High for 1 or 2 more minutes. Remove and stir until smooth.

Hot Fudge Sundae Sauce

Makes 1¼ cups sauce

Have you ever wished you had a generous spoonful of dark, delicious, hot fudge sauce to drizzle over ice cream or a brownie? With this recipe on hand, your wishes are answered—any time of the day or night.

> 1½ cups unsweetened cocoa powder
> ⅓ cup sugar
> ¼ cup packed brown sugar

½ cup heavy cream
4 tablespoons (2 ounces) butter, cut into pieces
1 tablespoon coffee liqueur
1 teaspoon vanilla extract

Combine the cocoa with both the sugars in a 1-quart glass measure. Stir in the cream, butter and liqueur. Microwave on High (100 percent) for 2 to 3 minutes until thickened, stirring every 50 or 60 seconds. Stir in the vanilla.

Serve the sauce hot or at room temperature.

Microwaving is the perfect way of reheating chocolate sauce. Store the sauce in a glass jar and there is no need to transfer it to any other container.

Chambord Deluxe Dessert Sauce

Makes about 2½ cups

A sophisticated version of raspberry sauce—try it with a lemon soufflé or chiffon pie.

> 15 ounces (1½ 10-ounce packages) frozen
>   raspberries, in syrup, thawed
> ¾ cup Chambord liqueur
> 3 tablespoons cornstarch
> 1½ tablespoons water
> 1½ tablespoons lemon juice

Drain the raspberries and save the syrup. Combine the syrup with the Chambord in a saucepan over medium-high heat and bring just to the boil.

Combine the cornstarch, water and lemon juice in a bowl. Stir into the raspberry syrup over low heat and cook, stirring, until the mixture is clear and thickened. Cover with transparent wrap and let the sauce cool to room temperature. Stir in the berries and serve.

Strawberry Sauce

Makes about 1 1/2 cups

For the best flavor
and texture, thaw
frozen straw-
berries and
raspberries in the
refrigerator . . .
slowly. Use
partially thawed
berries right
away; do not
refreeze them.

This is the sauce for the Lemonberry Saxon Pudding
on page 64, but it would be equally good with sliced
fresh fruit, lemon or lime sherbet—or ice cream of any
description.

> *20-ounce package whole frozen strawberries*
> *1/4 cup honey*
> *1/4 cup Amaretto (optional)*

Thaw the strawberries and press them through a fine
strainer to remove the seeds.

Put the strawberry puree in a bowl and add the honey
and Amaretto, if you are using it. Stir to blend and chill
until ready to serve.

Raspberry Sauce

Makes 1 cup

Raspberry sauce is always special because of its unique
tart-sweet flavor. Try it on lemon cake or poached
peaches as well as ice cream.

> *10-ounce package frozen raspberries in heavy*
> *syrup, defrosted*
> *2 tablespoons lemon juice*
> *1 tablespoon cornstarch*
> *2 tablespoons water*

Put the raspberries and lemon juice in a blender or
food processor and process until smooth. Press the
puree through a fine strainer to remove the seeds.

Pour the mixture into a 1-quart microwavable dish

and microwave on High (100 percent) for 2 to 2½ minutes, until boiling.

Stir the cornstarch and water together to form a smooth paste. Add this to the raspberry mixture, stirring to blend. Microwave on High (100 percent) for 1 to 2 minutes until the sauce is bubbling and thickened. Cover with transparent wrap and let cool.

Cherries Flambé

Makes 2 cups

This quickly made sauce can turn ice cream or crêpes into a dramatic dessert.

> ½ cup red currant jelly
> 1 tablespoon cornstarch
> 16-ounce can pitted dark sweet cherries, drained,
>   juice reserved
> 1 tablespoon lemon juice
> ¼ cup brandy

Spoon the jelly into a 1½-quart microwavable bowl. Microwave on High (100 percent) for 1 to 1½ minutes until the jelly is melted, stirring after 45 seconds.

Combine the cornstarch with ¼ cup of the reserved cherry juice and the lemon juice, stirring until smooth. Stir the juice mixture into the melted jelly. Microwave on High (100 percent) for 45 to 60 seconds until the mixture boils, stirring after 30 seconds. Stir in the cherries and microwave on High (100 percent) for 30 seconds to heat through.

Pour the brandy into a glass dish. Microwave on High (100 percent) for 20 to 25 seconds to warm it. Pour the warm brandy into a heatproof ladle or cup, carefully ignite and pour it, flaming, over the cherries. Serve the sauce immediately.

Igniting brandy or another spirit burns off the alcohol and leaves only the intense flavor.

Bananas Foster

Makes 2 cups

Bananas cooked in a sugary spiced sauce make a deliciously decadent topping for ice cream.

> *4 tablespoons (2 ounces) butter*
> *¼ cup packed brown sugar*
> *2 tablespoons orange juice*
> *2 tablespoons lemon juice*
> *¼ teaspoon cinnamon*
> *4 bananas, cut into pieces*
> *3 tablespoons brandy*

Put the butter in a 1½-quart microwavable bowl and microwave on High (100 percent) for 30 seconds or until melted. Stir in the brown sugar, orange juice, lemon juice and cinnamon. Microwave on High (100 percent) for 2 to 3 minutes until the mixture is hot and the sugar is dissolved.

Add the bananas to the sugar mixture, stirring well to coat. Microwave on High (100 percent) for 30 seconds to heat through.

Put the brandy in a small glass dish. Microwave on High (100 percent) for 20 to 25 seconds to warm it. Pour the brandy into a heatproof ladle or cup, carefully ignite and pour it, flaming, over the bananas. Serve the sauce immediately over ice cream.

Butterscotch Topping

Makes 2 cups

> *1 cup packed brown sugar*
> *½ cup dark corn syrup*

½ cup heavy cream
4 tablespoons (2 ounces) butter
5 tablespoons coffee liqueur

Combine the sugar, corn syrup, cream and butter in a 4-cup glass measure. Microwave on High (100 percent) for 3 to 3½ minutes until the mixture boils, stirring after 2 minutes.

Stir the coffee liqueur into the sauce and allow it to cool. Cover the sauce with transparent wrap and store it in the refrigerator.

A creamy smooth topping just right for ice cream, poached fruit or plain pound cake.

Hot Buttered Rum-Raisin Sauce

Makes 1¼ cups

Rum and raisins go together like peaches and cream and this sauce is absolutely divine served warm over ice cream or bread pudding.

2 tablespoons sugar
2 tablespoons packed brown sugar
1 tablespoon cornstarch
⅛ teaspoon salt
¾ cup water
⅓ cup dark rum
½ cup raisins
1 tablespoon butter

Combine both the sugars, the cornstarch and the salt in a 1-quart microwavable bowl. Stir in the water and rum. Microwave on High (100 percent) for 3 minutes or until thickened, stirring after 1½ minutes.

Stir in the raisins and the butter. Microwave on High (100 percent) for 1 minute. Stir again before serving.

Festive Whipped Cream

Makes about 1 cup

A dressed-up version of whipped cream that is especially good with chocolate cream pie and poached peaches or pears.

>*½ cup heavy cream*
>*2 tablespoons confectioners' sugar*
>*1–2 teaspoons bourbon or ½ teaspoon vanilla*
>*   extract*

Whip the cream with the sugar in a chilled bowl until frothy. Add the bourbon or vanilla extract and beat until stiff peaks form. Serve at once.

Hard Sauce

Makes about 2½ cups

Hard sauce is the traditional partner to Christmas plum pudding—and with good reason!

>*1 cup (½ pound) unsalted butter*
>*2 cups confectioners' sugar*
>*⅓ cup Amaretto or brandy*

Beat the butter and sugar together in a large mixing bowl until light and fluffy. Gradually beat in the Amaretto or brandy. Chill the hard sauce until firm.

INDEX